SURVIVORS

INSPIRING TRUE STORIES OF SURVIVAL

THIS IS A MORTIMER CHILDREN'S BOOK

Published in 2021 by Mortimer Children's Books,
an imprint of Welbeck Children's Limited,
part of Welbeck Publishing Group
20 Mortimer Street London W1T 3JW

ISBN: 978-1-83935-065-8

Printed in Dongguan, China

10 9 8 7 6 5 4 3 2 1

Illustrated by: Neil@KJA-artists.com
Supplemental art: Intrepid Studios
Design and illustration by: Jacob Da'Costa & !ntrepid Books Ltd.
Design Manager: Emily Clarke
Commissioning Editor: Bryony Davies
Production: Marion Storz
Picture Research: Paul Langan

The publishers would like to thank the following sources for their kind permission to
reproduce the pictures in this book. T = top; l = left; c = center; r = right; b = bottom

PA IMAGES: /Darren Calabrese/The Canadian Press: 23B; /Eventpress Stauffenberg/
DPA: 75

GETTY IMAGES: /New York Daily News Archive: 37BR; /Vera Anderson: 47BR; /AFP/
Stringer: 49BR; /Rolls Press/Popperfoto: 59BR

SHUTTERSTOCK: /Here: background textures throughout; /Janaka Dharmasena:
background textures throughout; /Amovitania: background textures throughout; Picsfive:
background textures throughout; /Itsmesimon: background textures throughout plus
additional texture on 8-9, 12-13, 16-17, 20-21, 24-25, 28-29, 36-37, 40-41, 44-45,
48-49, 52-53, 56-57, 60-61, 64-65, 68-69, 70-71, 72-73, 76-77, 80-81, 84-85; /Miloje
(text background): 10C, 11B, 14T, 15, 16T, 17R, 26C, 27BL, 30BR, 31BL, 34C, 35BL, 38C,
39C, 46B, 47CR, 52B, 56BR, 61C, 63BR, 67BR, 78B, 79BR, 80CR, 83BR, 84B, 85CR,
92-96; /Photology1971 (texture): 10-11, 14-15, 18-19, 22-23, 26-27, 30-31, 34-35, 38-39,
42-43, 46-47, 50-51, 54-55, 58-59, 62-63, 66-67, 70-71, 74-75, 78-79, 82-83, 86-87;
/Picsfive (paper background): 18, 22, 25BR, 37BR, 42L, 50C, 54BR, 58C, 73BR, 86BR;
/humbak (lined paper background): 20C, 29BR, 32C, 39CR, 41TR, 57TR, 60B, 72TR,
81BR; /1494 (texture): 29TR, 36-37, 40-41, 44-45, 46-47, 48-49, 52-53, 56-57, 58-59,
60-61, 64-65, 68-69, 72-73, 74-75, 76-77, 78-79, 80-81, 84-85; /Pat Wellenbach/AP/
Shutterstock: 31BR; /FL Wong (texture): 40-41, 64-65, 76-77; /Milan M: 88-89, 90-91

Every effort has been made to acknowledge correctly and contact the source and/or
copyright holder of each picture. Any unintentional errors or omissions will be corrected
in future editions of this book.

SURVIVORS

INSPIRING TRUE STORIES OF SURVIVAL

Written by Ben Hubbard

MORTIMER

Contents

Introduction

What does it mean to be a survivor? The survivors in this book are all people who overcame great obstacles during a time of danger, disaster, or personal peril. Their stories are surprising, scary, inspiring, and sometimes upsetting.

Some survivors lived through ship, airplane, and spacecraft wrecks, only to find the true struggle to survive had just begun. Some of the survivors found themselves stranded at sea, in the jungle, or in the Sahara desert. Some walked for days on broken legs with maggot-infested wounds or drank urine and bat's blood to stay alive.

Perhaps the most inspirational survivors are those who did not spare a second thought for themselves but instead put the lives of others first. They are the heroes who plunged through fire and floodwater to rescue those around them.

What would you do to survive? Some of the survivors in this book had to hit rock bottom before they found out. Lost, alone, and with no help in sight, they summoned a new strength from somewhere deep inside in order to keep going. They fought to stay alive—even when they lost limbs in the process.

This is why reading the stories of survivors is so interesting. We immediately wonder what we would do in the same situation. Would we fight back, or would we give up? Perhaps it is impossible to know until we too are faced with great adversity. However, we can take heart from the survivors in the following pages. The thing that unites them is that in the end their desire to live outweighed all else. This book is about our ability to overcome seemingly impossible obstacles when the odds are stacked against us. It is a celebration of the human spirit.

SHARK ATTACK

Bethany Hamilton

On Halloween morning in 2003, Bethany Hamilton and three friends paddled out for a surf at Tunnels Beach in Kauai, Hawaii. Bethany lay face down on her surfboard about 600 feet (180 meters) from shore, her right arm dangling in the water. Then, without warning, disaster struck.

The ocean was clear and reasonably calm, but the surfers did not see a 15-foot-long (4.5-meter) tiger shark prowling below them. All were experienced surfers: 13-year-old Bethany had been surfing since she was four and had been sponsored from the age of nine.

Bethany suddenly felt a violent jolt as the tiger shark grabbed her shoulder and started jerking her from side to side. It felt, Bethany said, like "how you eat a piece of steak." Sharks commonly bite something to test whether it is worth eating. They also shake their prey to tear off chunks of flesh to eat.

Bethany held fast to her board with the other arm as she noticed the water around her turning red. Then, as suddenly as it had started, the attack stopped. The shark was gone, but so was Bethany's arm, shorn cleanly off from her shoulder.

The attack had been so fast that her friends had not even noticed. Bethany called out calmly: "I've been attacked by a shark." For a moment her friends thought she was joking.

One of Bethany's friends helped get her to shore as quickly as possible. On the beach, they used a surfboard leash as a tourniquet, tying it around her shoulder stump to slow the bleeding. But by the time help arrived, Bethany had lost almost 60 percent of her blood and was going into shock. The race was on to save her life.

> "I had this one pretty funny thought: 'I wonder if I'm going to lose my sponsor.'"
>
> *One of Bethany's first reactions to the shark attack*

TIGER SHARKS

Tiger sharks are often called the trash cans of the sea because they eat almost anything. Objects found in their stomachs include a porcupine, a drum, and a car license plate.

When Bethany arrived at nearby Wilcox Memorial Hospital, she was raced into surgery. By strange coincidence, hers was the operating room that her father was already waiting in to have knee surgery, scheduled for that same day. Luckily, a surgeon was staying at a nearby hotel, and he sped to Bethany's rescue. Her life was saved.

The whole attack had been so fast that nobody was sure how to react—that is, except for Bethany. The only thing on her mind was how soon she could get back into the water. She was determined not to let the loss of her arm crush her dream of becoming a professional surfer. Meanwhile, fishermen near Tunnels Beach reported catching a 15-foot (4.5-meter) tiger shark with pieces of surfboard lodged in its teeth. A police investigation showed the bite mark on Bethany's board was the same size as the caught shark's mouth. The threat was over.

Bethany was back in the ocean surfing only 26 days after the shark attack. She had to adapt her style by paddling more with her feet and using a thicker board with a handle. But the results were astounding. Two years after losing her arm, Bethany

> "If I don't get back on my board, I'll be in a bad mood forever."

won a surfing competition in Australia. The next year she won two further competitions in the United States. At 18 years old, Bethany turned professional.

The attack made Bethany into something of a celebrity shark survivor. This was a title she didn't like, as she felt it detracted from her status as a surfer. However, after appearing on numerous television talk shows to tell her story, Bethany found a way to give something back using her fame. She did this by starting a nonprofit organization called Friends of Bethany Hamilton, which helps children and young people who have had limbs amputated. Bethany has also written a book and is the subject of a documentary, *Bethany Hamilton: Unstoppable*, which was released in 2019.

SURVIVE A SHARK ATTACK

- Fight back by punching and kicking the shark in its eyes and gills.
- Swim back to shore as calmly as possible.
- Once on land, put pressure anywhere that is bleeding and seek immediate medical help.

LOST INSIDE A MOUNTAIN

The Thai Cave Boys

Saturday, June 23, 2018, was a special day for the junior Wild Boars soccer team of Chiang Rai, Thailand. Peerapat, one of their teammates, was turning 17. As a treat after practice, the team rode their bikes out to explore the nearby Tham Luang cave. But once the boys were inside, disaster struck.

The Wild Boars often visited Tham Luang, a 6-mile-long (10-kilometer) cave system that lies under the towering mountain range nearby. The boys agreed to only be an hour, so Peerapat would not be late for his birthday dinner. The cave was dry as the boys walked deep inside; but then, suddenly, water began to flow in.

There had been heavy rainfall over the mountains for several weeks, and now that water was flooding the cave. It rose too quickly for the boys to get back to the entrance, so they had to go further inside, finding refuge on a sandy shelf called Pattaya Beach. With water lapping at their feet, the 12 boys and their 25-year-old coach, Ekkapol "Ake" Chantawong, were trapped.

Ake taught the boys meditation techniques so they would preserve their strength and not panic. Clean water was falling from the cave's ceiling for the boys to drink. The cold and the lack of food and a toilet were their most immediate problems.

Outside the cave, the alarm was soon raised. The boys' bikes were found at the cave's entrance, and local authorities, including Thai Navy SEALs (special operations forces), were soon on the scene. It was clear that rescuing the boys would require a diving operation. But the water was still rising, flooding most of the cave's chambers and making the chance of a rescue remote.

"We only had a little bit of hope that they might be alive . . . in the end that tiny bit of hope became a reality."

Thai Navy SEAL leader Arpakorn Yuukongkaew on the cave rescue

THAM LUANG CAVE

The Tham Luang cave only officially reopened in November 2019, but the site around the entrance became an instant attraction for tourists after the Wild Boars became trapped there.

SURVIVE IN A CAVE

Rockfalls and flash floods can catch cavers unawares. Here's what to do:

- Move to the highest point in the cave and keep as dry as possible.
- Wring out your clothes if they are wet.
- Look for clean drinking water coming through the rock above you. Don't drink still or stagnant water.

Large industrial pumps were brought in to pump some of the fast-moving water out of the cave. Meanwhile, locals set up a makeshift camp to feed rescuers and helpers. The rescue became a community effort, with over 7,000 people giving their time and personal funds to help. But now the boys had been missing for over a week, and some families were beginning to fear the worst.

Expert cave divers came from around the world. Navigating the small submerged chambers in the dark against the strong current was perilously dangerous. But as multiple teams spent hours laying a guide rope through the caves, a British team made an incredible discovery. Just beyond Pattaya Beach was a small air pocket, and here the Wild Boars sat huddled together.

After talking to the boys, the divers returned to the cave entrance to deliver the good news. More divers, including a doctor, then swam through to the boys with food and supplies. However, this was still dangerous: an experienced Navy SEAL, Saman Gunan, died while doing so. How, therefore, would 12 boys between 11 and 17 years old be able to make the dive?

A plan was formed to give each boy a sedative and cover their face with an oxygen mask. They would then be clipped to a diver who would swim them both through the flooded cave. It was extremely risky, but they had to act quickly: the oxygen where the boys were trapped was running out. It took five hours for the first boy to be reunited with his family, but the rest of the team soon followed. The Wild Boars had been saved.

> "We were faced with an impossible decision. Stay where they were and they are all going to die. If we brought them out, there was a chance some might survive. It was the Devil and the deep blue sea."
>
> *British diver John Volanthen*

VIETNAMESE AIR CRASHES

About half the surface area of Vietnam is covered with jungle. The country has a humid, tropical climate with heavy rainfall during the monsoon season. Rainstorms were partly to blame for at least two of the five air crashes in Vietnam between 1988 and 2010.

RAINFOREST RESCUE

Annette Herfkens

When Annette Herfkens saw the plane awaiting her was an aging Soviet-made Yakovlev Yak-40, she didn't want to get on board. But her boyfriend assured her that everything would be all right. After all, the flight to the tropical beaches of Nha Trang, Vietnam, would only take an hour. But the plane would never make it that far.

The vacation to Nha Trang in 1992 had been a romantic surprise from Annette's boyfriend, Pasje. But as soon as Annette got on board Flight 474, she began to feel anxious. Pasje, too, looked nervous when the plane dropped suddenly while flying over the Vietnamese jungle. There was a roar as the plane's engine accelerated. When the plane dropped again, the passengers started screaming. The plane hurtled toward the ground. Everything went black for Annette.

> "I could see four inches of bluish bone sticking out through layers of flesh on my shin."

At first the plane had met heavy turbulence, but then it had clipped a mountain and some treetops. One of the plane's wings had broken off, spinning it toward another mountain—which made it flip upside down. As it crashed into the jungle below, the plane all but disintegrated. Most of the passengers died immediately.

When Annette came to, she noticed an eerie silence and then the sounds of the jungle. She had not been wearing her seatbelt and had been tossed around the cabin. She was pinned to the floor by one of the seats, which had come loose. Belted into the seat was one of the other passengers, now a body.

Annette managed to push away the seat and find Pasje. He had not made it. She was struck by the horror of her situation; she was surrounded by dead people in the middle of the jungle, with no help in sight.

Annette could hear the moans of some of the other survivors as she lowered herself from the broken fuselage onto the jungle floor. She had broken her leg in two places, fractured her hip, and broken her jaw. One of her lungs had also collapsed. Before long, all of the other passengers died. Now Annette was the only survivor of the 30 people on board the plane.

Unable to move except for crawling on her elbows, Annette survived for several days by drinking rainwater from a leaf. By the eighth day, Annette's kidneys were starting to fail and her wounds were becoming gangrenous (decaying). Then, as she slipped in and out of consciousness, she was rescued.

At first, the Vietnamese policeman who discovered Annette thought she was a ghost. When he recovered his senses, he alerted his colleagues and together they carried Annette to the nearest village on a stretcher.

> "Pasje and I had been together for 13 years, so it felt like I was widowed. I attended his funeral ... on a stretcher. I felt surreal—like a bride taken down the aisle to meet her groom in his coffin."

After she had recuperated, Annette spent many months giving interviews about her ordeal. She also wrote a best-selling memoir about her experience. In 2006, Annette returned to visit the site of the crash and mourn Pasje's death.

SURVIVE IN THE JUNGLE

- Keep looking up as well as all around you: you're as likely to die from a falling branch as a snake bite.
- Build shelter and fire while it's still light —it gets dark very quickly.
- Protect your skin against disease-carrying mosquitoes with insect repellent and long clothes at all times.

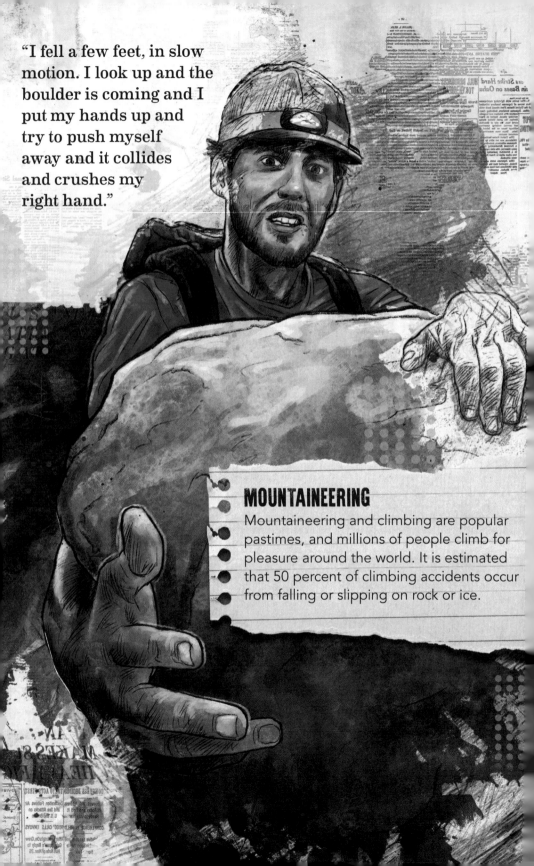

"I fell a few feet, in slow motion. I look up and the boulder is coming and I put my hands up and try to push myself away and it collides and crushes my right hand."

MOUNTAINEERING

Mountaineering and climbing are popular pastimes, and millions of people climb for pleasure around the world. It is estimated that 50 percent of climbing accidents occur from falling or slipping on rock or ice.

TRAPPED IN A CANYON

Aron Ralston

On the fifth day of being stuck in a canyon, Aron Ralston decided he was going to die. He recorded goodbyes to family and friends on his camcorder and showed them the 800-pound (360-kilogram) boulder that had fallen on his wrist, trapping him there. Aron could not escape, and his arm was decomposing. The end seemed near.

On April 26, 2003, 27-year-old Aron Ralston decided to take a daylong hike in Utah's Bluejohn Canyon. An experienced outdoorsman, Aron had prepared a backpack with two burritos, a bottle of water, some chocolate, a camcorder, and a cheap multi-tool, which contained a short blade and pliers. As he began climbing down a very narrow canyon, he dislodged a boulder. He slipped down the canyon's sides and the boulder followed. It fell heavily on his right wrist, crushing it against the wall.

Aron tried everything he could to free his arm, but the boulder would not budge. He cut away at the boulder's edges with his short multi-tool blade and tried to lift it with his climbing ropes. Nothing worked. He did not have a phone, nor had he told anyone where he was going. At the bottom of the narrow canyon, Aron would not be seen from the air.

Aron spent three days trying to break away from the boulder and rationing his food supplies. When his water ran out, he drank his own urine. Aron had no sensation in his right arm, which had turned a sickening grayish-blue. He had not been able to sit down properly for days and was exhausted from lack of sleep and food. His eyes stung from the desert grit, and his mouth was parched and sore from drinking urine.

Dehydrated, delirious, and dangerously unwell, Aron accepted that no one was coming to rescue him. He recorded goodbye messages on his camcorder, and then Aron began to hallucinate. He imagined himself as an older man, balancing his son on his right arm, half of which was missing. When he came around, Aron knew that he had to amputate his own arm.

Using his knife to brush away some sand from his trapped hand, Aron accidently sliced off a sliver from his thumb, which came away easily. His blunt knife would cut through flesh, but there was no way it would cut through solid bone.

Aron realized that he could use the boulder to break his arm bones. He began to yank and twist his arm until he heard his bones crack. He then tied a climbing rope around his upper arm as a tourniquet and began to cut through the skin, tendons, and nerves on his arm using the knife and pliers. The operation took an hour but, by the end, Aron was free.

Aron climbed out of the canyon, rappelled down a 65-foot (20-meter) wall and walked the 21 miles (34 kilometers) out of the canyon, all one-handed. He then came across a family from the Netherlands who gave him water and alerted the authorities. Soon, Aron was being helicoptered to a nearby hospital. He had survived his ordeal.

Later, the authorities reclaimed Aron's arm: they needed 13 men, a winch, and a jackhammer to remove the boulder. It took Aron himself many months to recover, but when he did he was a celebrity. Since then he has written a best-selling book and is the subject of a movie, *127 Hours*. Today he continues to hike and mountaineer around the world.

"The knife just slips into the meat of my thumb like it's going into room-temperature butter. My hand has almost jellified. The knife tip goes in and, 'pssstt,' the gases from decomposition escape and there's this putrid smell."

SURVIVE AS A CLIMBER
- Always tell someone where you are going and never climb alone.
- Take enough provisions and warm clothes to last a week of being lost.
- Always wear a helmet and harness and check your climbing knots carefully.

THE SAHARA DESERT

Covering an area of almost 3.3 million square miles (8.6 million square kilometers) across North Africa, the Sahara is the largest desert in the world. It is home to around 2.5 million people, including the Tuareg Berber people.

MISSING IN THE DESERT

Mauro Prosperi

The sandstorm struck Sahara runner Mauro Prosperi and enveloped him. Sand whipped his face, and everything went black. Forced to keep moving or be buried, Mauro finally found a place to shelter. The storm raged for eight hours. When it passed, Mauro was lost.

The Marathon des Sables is a notoriously tough six-day run across 155 miles (250 kilometers) of the Sahara desert. It's considered the ultimate endurance test. Today, around 1,300 runners enter the race each year, but in 1994, the year the 39-year-old Italian policeman entered, there were only 80 runners.

Mauro was carrying his own food and tent, so he would not go hungry, for now. But he had been given his last bottle of water when he had passed the last manned checkpoint. By the time the storm was over, it was only half full. He urinated into a bottle, thinking that while he was still hydrated it would contain the most drinking water. He then set off, heeding some advice he had previously been given that if he got lost, he should set his compass toward the morning clouds and then walk in that direction.

On the second day at sunset, a helicopter appeared. It came close enough that Mauro could see the pilot's helmet. He fired a flare into the sky, but the helicopter did not see him. All Mauro could then do was hope that the race organizers were looking for him.

"My wife, Cinzia, thought I was insane ... I tried to reassure her. 'The worst that can happen is that I get a bit sunburned,' I said."

Mauro responding to his wife's concerns on being told he was entering the race

Eventually, Mauro came across a marabout (shrine). Here he rested and made a meal of dehydrated food cooked in urine. Then he noticed some bats huddled in the corner. He mashed up their insides with his knife. This disgusting concoction sustained Mauro for a few days in the marabout.

The next day, Mauro heard a plane and quickly made a signal fire. But once again, he was not seen. Now he started to despair. But the next morning, Mauro became determined to rescue himself. He had some energy tablets and some of his bottled urine left, so he set out. He walked for days, killing snakes and lizards and eating them raw.

Meanwhile, the race organizers were looking for Mauro; they had found his shoelaces in the marabout and now felt sure they would be searching for a body. But Mauro was not going to die in the desert.

On the eighth day, he came across an oasis. Mauro fell by the waters and stayed there sipping the water for over six hours. He then noticed a footprint in the sand leading to goats, a young shepherd girl, and a tent. The women in the tent fed Mauro goat's milk and called the police. After surviving 10 days in the desert and walking 180 miles (290 kilometers) off course, Mauro Prosperi was saved.

"Desert fever does exist, and it's a disease that I've absolutely caught. I'm drawn back to the desert every year to greet it, to experience it."

Mauro had lost 35 pounds (16 kilograms) in weight and had eye and liver damage: it would take him two whole years to recover. But four years later, Mauro was back running the Marathon des Sables. "People ask me why I went back, but when I start something I want to finish it," he said.

SURVIVE IN THE DESERT
- Urine contains salt and urea that are dehydrating—avoid drinking it.
- Drinking another animal's blood will help hydrate you.

SHIPWRECKED AT SEA

Steven Callahan

Steven Callahan was expecting a weeklong Atlantic storm as he battened down the hatches and tried to sleep. Then, as winds buffeted his *Napoleon Solo* sloop, there was an explosion: something had torn open the hull. Cold seawater poured over Steven in his bunk.

Steven jumped from his bunk into water that was already waist-deep around him. He felt fear, panic, and even amusement all at once, but then his survival instinct kicked in. He started to inflate his life raft above deck, but quickly realized his most important supplies were still in the submerged cabin below him. He made several dives to retrieve important items. In the flooded cabin the water was calm, but back above the surface the storm raged.

Steven tied a rope from his raft to the part of *Napoleon Solo* that was still above the surface. He then collapsed into the raft, exhausted. All night, waves beat the canopy of Steven's 6-foot (1.8-meter) raft. He was forced to use a tin can to bail out the water rapidly filling the bottom. Sometime before dawn, the rope between the raft and *Napoleon Solo* broke. Steven was now on his own, adrift in the middle of the Atlantic Ocean.

Steven calculated he was around 800 miles (1,300 kilometers) west of the Canary Islands, but heading away from land. He also recorded the date in a logbook: February 5, 1982. Steven had set out in *Napoleon Solo*, which he had built from scratch, to race across the Atlantic. However, after eight days he had dropped out of the race to make his own way. Then the collision had taken place, which Steven believed was with a whale. Now, with food and water for only 14 days, he was in a race for his survival.

"In the coming days, I had a lot of time to think, and I regretted every mistake I'd ever made—I was divorced, and felt I had failed at human relations generally, at business, and now even at sailing."

THE ATLANTIC OCEAN

The Atlantic Ocean covers around 20 percent of the world's surface. It is the site of innumerable shipwrecks, including *Titanic*, which sank after hitting an iceberg in 1912, with the loss of more than 1,500 passengers.

Luckily, Steven had rescued some equipment from his boat, including a speargun and solar stills to make drinking water. On day 13, as his food supplies ran low, Steven caught a triggerfish. He thought he would soon be entering the Atlantic shipping lanes and have a chance of being rescued. Ships did appear on the horizon, but none responded to his flares.

Steven kept himself busy by manufacturing water and catching fish to eat. However, after around six weeks, he broke his fishing spear. The broken spear sliced a hole in a watertight compartment in the raft that kept his supplies dry. For more than a week, Steven tried to repair the hole in the raft but failed. To keep the raft afloat he had to constantly pump it up with a hand pump. As his solar stills started producing less water, the raft drifted into more tropical waters, making his growing thirst harder to tolerate. He was hungry, thirsty, and covered in saltwater sores. After 50 days at sea, Steven felt ready to give up.

At his lowest ebb, Steven decided to try fixing the raft once again and managed to patch it up successfully. This gave him the strength to try to stay alive. Three weeks later, three fishermen aboard a boat from Guadeloupe saw seabirds hovering around Steven's raft. They were feeding on fish remains from Steven's catches. When the boat picked Steven up, he had lost more than a third of his body weight and was suffering from severe dehydration. It would take six weeks of being on dry land for Steven to recover the strength to walk again. Today, Steven Callahan, the man who was shipwrecked at sea for 76 days, is alive and well and continues to sail.

"I really did lie down and think about giving up for a while, but decided 'no' and went through my gear and made it work."

SURVIVE AT SEA

The right equipment can be vital in the fight for survival at sea. Steven Callahan had a few key items:

- A speargun for fishing
- A solar still which uses the sun's heat to evaporate and distill salt water
- A raft-patching kit.

CALIFORNIA WILDFIRES

In 2018 more than 8,500 fires ravaged an area of 2,953 square miles (7,649 square kilometers) and led to over $12 billion worth of damage. The Camp Fire, which devastated northern California's Butte County, claimed 85 lives.

ESCAPE FROM A WILDFIRE

Allyn Pierce

As nurse Allyn Pierce and several of his hospital colleagues sat stuck in Allyn's truck, flames began to scorch the side of the vehicle. The heat was so intense that it melted the truck's side-view mirrors. Allyn tried to calm everyone with music, but it seemed unlikely that any of them would survive the raging wildfire outside.

When Allyn arrived at Feather River Hospital in Paradise, California, on the morning of November 8, 2018, the sky was filled with a thick, orange haze. Parts of California had been struck by intense wildfires during July of that year. But in November strong winds had aggravated conditions and the wildfires had spread.

The wildfire that broke out in Paradise was particularly bad. Here the flames would virtually destroy the whole town, burning down more than 18,000 buildings and homes in the process. It would become the most destructive fire in California's history, and when Allyn arrived at work, it had only just begun.

The wildfire had not yet reached the hospital, but the advice was to remove everyone as quickly as possible. Allyn and his team immediately evacuated the few dozen patients at the hospital by ambulance. By 9:30 a.m, the hospital was empty except for a few staff members.

Allyn ordered these staff members into his Toyota Tundra pickup truck and made a getaway. He decided to drive to the closest highway by taking a nearby gully road. The problem was that the

"Take pics, this is the last time I'll be doing this tour!"

gully was on fire, and many other drivers had also had the same idea as Allyn. Now they were all stuck in gridlocked traffic. Ahead, a couple of fuel tanks exploded and a nearby car caught fire. His passengers got out and sheltered in a nearby firetruck, while Allyn held up a coat to his window against the heat. Then he recorded a goodbye message to his family on his phone.

Just as things looked their bleakest, there was a crash next to Allyn's truck. A bulldozer had smashed an empty vehicle in front of him out of the way. Now Allyn could turn his truck around and speed away. He decided to go back to the hospital, which to his amazement was still standing. Emergency workers, including firefighters and police officers, were outside tending to people who had been caught in the fire.

Allyn sprang into action, setting up an area outside the hospital with supplies from inside. Soon the hospital parking lot looked like an emergency room, and Allyn and his colleagues began treating people for smoke inhalation and burns. This continued for several hours, until the fire came too close to the hospital. Those at the hospital decided on a second site they could set up as an emergency hospital, and once again Allyn found himself evacuating people in his truck. This time, they took a route not yet affected by the wildfire, and Allyn was able to evacuate his passengers without incident.

> "I was calm because I'm a nurse, and that's what we do. But I was terrified . . . I really did think I was going to die."

Later, when Allyn was tearfully reunited with his family, he inspected the damage to his truck. The heat of the fire had melted his taillights and welded a rear door shut. Scorch marks along the truck's sides made it look like a toasted marshmallow. After hearing Allyn's story and seeing comments on social media about the truck saving his life, Toyota offered to give Allyn a new truck. In return, Allyn donated his fire-damaged truck to them, so they could show what it could withstand.

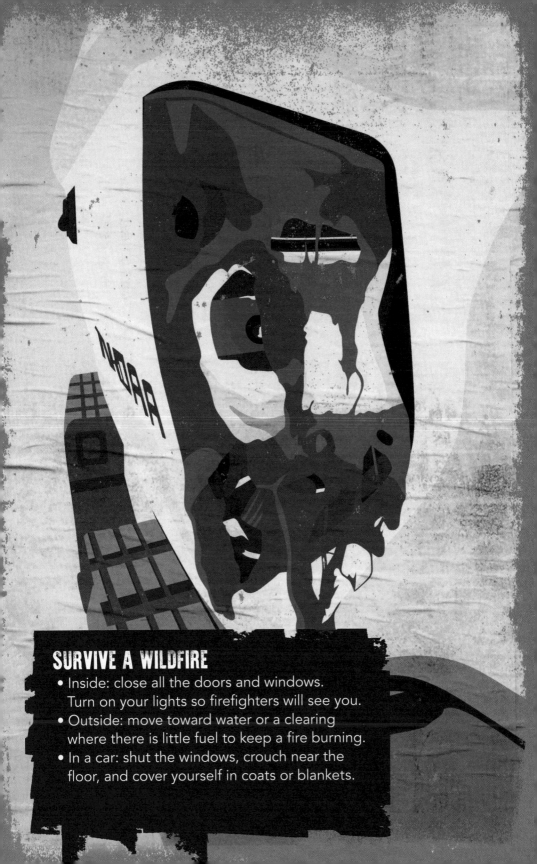

SURVIVE A WILDFIRE

- Inside: close all the doors and windows. Turn on your lights so firefighters will see you.
- Outside: move toward water or a clearing where there is little fuel to keep a fire burning.
- In a car: shut the windows, crouch near the floor, and cover yourself in coats or blankets.

MIRACLE ON THE HUDSON

Chesley Sullenberger

US Airways Flight 1549 was traveling at an altitude of 2,800 feet (850 meters) on January 15, 2009, when it collided with a flock of Canada geese. Both engines burst into flames, and the plane began losing power. As it plummeted toward the ground, the pilot had only minutes to find a place to crash-land.

Captain Chesley "Sully" Sullenberger III made a Mayday distress call to air traffic control at LaGuardia, the New York airport they had taken off from only minutes earlier. He explained his plane had lost power and that he would try to return to LaGuardia.

But the plane was not going to make it that far, so he changed his mind. It was dropping at 18 feet (5.5 meters) a second, and all Chesley could do was try to glide it down to the safest place. His problem was not only the 150 passengers onboard the plane, but also the residents of Manhattan, toward whom the plane was careering. Chesley made a split-second decision: "We're going to be in the Hudson," he reported to air traffic control.

It was now clear to the plane's passengers that something was wrong. One reported the engines making a strange thudding sound "like gym shoes in a dryer." Outside the window, the city's skyline could be seen getting lower. Then an announcement was made: "This is the captain. Brace for impact."

Astonished onlookers in Manhattan began calling emergency services, reporting a plane falling toward the Hudson River. It was heading for the enormous George Washington Bridge— but Chesley managed to guide it just 650 feet (200 meters) over the bridge and then pull back the plane's tail to lessen the impact.

"No, too low. Too slow. Too many buildings. Too populated an area."

Captain Sullenberger rejects air traffic control's suggestion of landing back at LaGuardia Airport.

CHESLEY SULLENBERGER

Born January 23, 1951, Captain Chesley Sullenberger III had been a pilot for over 30 years when he landed in the Hudson River. He retired a year later to become a speaker on airline safety, and he cowrote a best-selling memoir of his experiences.

The plane hit the frigid January river at a descent rate three times higher than the plane could handle. Passengers reported that the plane "groaned" as the fuselage cracked at its rear and a deluge of icy water rushed in. All 150 passengers had survived the crash but were now in a new race for their lives.

The plane took on water fast and would not stay afloat for long. As passengers waded toward the emergency exits, some jumped from the plane's wings into the water. At only about 35°F (2°C), the water was perilously cold: those now in it would perish if they stayed submerged for long.

An emergency helicopter and scuba divers were scrambled to attend the crashed plane, but the first people to arrive at the scene were Hudson River ferry boats. The boats threw life jackets and rope ladders for passengers to climb up. But the situation

"It doesn't get any better than to have Tom Hanks portray you in a movie."

quickly became chaotic, and one of the ferries almost crushed one of the plane's inflatable rafts.

Meanwhile, two scuba divers dived into the Hudson to search for survivors still stuck onboard. Chesley, one of the last people to leave the plane, reported he had twice checked the cabin. In the end, every passenger survived, although five serious injuries occurred during the landing, and several people were treated for hypothermia.

Chesley Sullenberger won many accolades and awards for what was described as "the most successful ditching in aviation history" and the "miracle on the Hudson River." Chesley's skill and quick thinking was recounted in many media interviews and even the eponymous movie *Sully*, starring Tom Hanks.

SURVIVE A PLANE CRASH

- Wear sensible shoes and comfortable clothes that will keep you warm.
- Count the rows between you and the exit in case there's too much smoke to see after a crash.
- If in a crash, leave your possessions and move at least 500 feet (150 m) away from the plane.

EXTREME ERUPTION

Venus Dergan and Roald Reitan

Venus Dergan and Roald Reitan didn't hear Mount St. Helens erupt, about 30 miles (48 kilometers) from their campsite. They awoke to a mass of water, mud, and debris crashing down the mountainside toward them. The couple threw their tent in their car and jumped onto the roof, just as it was swept away.

On the morning of May 18, 1980, Venus, 19, and Roald, 20, were on a quiet fishing trip by the Toutle River in the state of Washington. Nearby Mount St. Helens had been rumbling for several weeks, but the couple had chosen a spot 10 miles (16 kilometers) outside the government's evacuation zone. They assumed that if the volcano erupted, they would be safe. They were wrong.

At 8:32 a.m., a 5.1 magnitude earthquake triggered a gigantic landslide on the north face of Mount St. Helens. As the slope fell away, the volcano erupted from its side, blasting a cloud of searing ash, gas, and rock 15 miles (24 kilometers) over the landscape below. Moving at over 300 mph (480 kmh) and reaching temperatures of over 660°F (350°C), the devastating cloud incinerated trees and claimed most of the 57 lives lost that day.

Venus and Roald were too far away to be in danger from the landslide or the blast, but not the lahar—a fast-moving mixture of volcanic debris, mud, and water—that followed. Caused by rapid melting of the mountain's ice and snow, the lahar picked up speed as it crashed down the mountain valley toward the couple's campsite. The lahar had picked up a large stack of logs stored at a timber hut on the way down, making it even more dangerous. Venus and Roald were now in imminent peril.

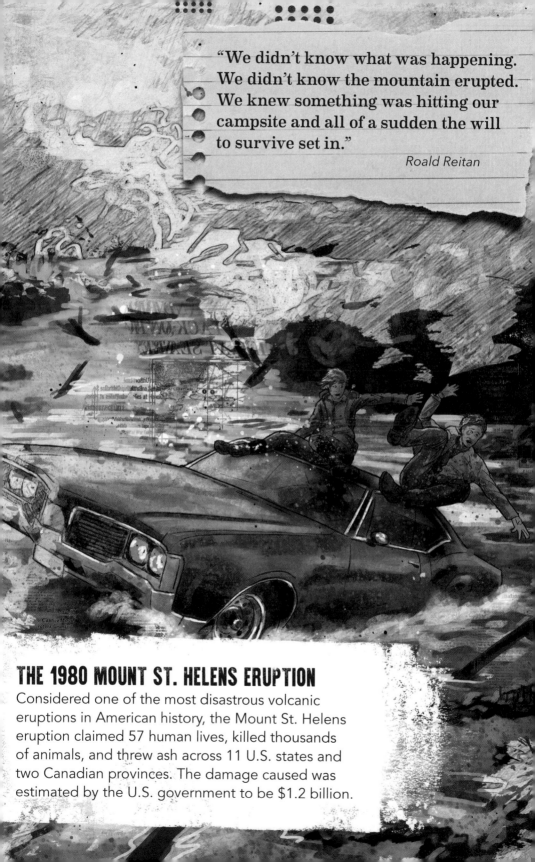

"We didn't know what was happening. We didn't know the mountain erupted. We knew something was hitting our campsite and all of a sudden the will to survive set in."

Roald Reitan

THE 1980 MOUNT ST. HELENS ERUPTION

Considered one of the most disastrous volcanic eruptions in American history, the Mount St. Helens eruption claimed 57 human lives, killed thousands of animals, and threw ash across 11 U.S. states and two Canadian provinces. The damage caused was estimated by the U.S. government to be $1.2 billion.

As the lahar struck Venus and Roald's car, the couple tried desperately to cling on to its roof. But the car started to turn in the rapid flow of the lahar, and the couple were thrown off. The mud, water, and debris of the lahar had the consistency of chocolate syrup. As Venus fell into it, she was immediately sucked under.

Roald, meanwhile, managed to climb onto a log and tried to locate his girlfriend. He saw Venus's nose poke out between two logs for an instant, and he grabbed her, pulling her onto his log. Venus's arm had been badly crushed between logs caught up in the lahar's flow; she was lucky to be alive.

The log carrying the couple then swept them half a mile (1 kilometer) downstream and onto a riverbank. They climbed a steep hillside and came out onto a road at the top. They were soon airlifted to a hospital, where they learned that they had survived one of the greatest American volcanic eruptions in living memory.

The couple spent several weeks in the hospital recovering: Venus's wrist had been fractured, and she needed skin grafts to replace the skin torn away by the logs. Roald's knee had been badly damaged.

After a few weeks, the couple visited what was left of the area around their campsite. They found their car several miles downstream, buried nose-down in the ground—only the trunk was left sticking out.

> "When you're 20 years old, you think you're immortal, and you don't think about your mortality. We got a slap in the face of our mortality that day."
> *Venus Dergan*

Scattered around the car were its parts and contents, ripped away during the journey downstream. These included its license plates, Roald's rifle, and Venus's purse. To their delight, the couple found an unopened bottle of champagne still inside the trunk. With this, they were able to toast their good fortune at having survived this natural disaster.

SURVIVE A VOLCANO

- Run, find shelter, and protect your head and neck from falling projectiles.
- Keep away from low-lying areas that lahars and lava might run down: stay on ridges.
- Cover your mouth with a damp cloth to reduce the amount of toxic gas and ash you breathe in.

LOST AT SEA

Tami Oldham Ashcraft

The last thing that Tami Oldham Ashcraft heard before being knocked unconscious was her fiancé Richard Sharp shout out "Oh my god!" When she came to 27 hours later, Tami was surrounded by debris and seawater in the cabin of their yacht. Richard was gone. Now Tami was alone and adrift in the Pacific Ocean.

Tami and Richard were both experienced sailors who had jumped at the chance of sailing the 44-foot (13.4-meter) yacht *Hazana* 4,000 miles (6,400 kilometers) between Tahiti and San Diego, California, in October 1983. But three weeks into the voyage, the couple met a Category 4 hurricane. To maneuver the yacht through the storm, Richard clipped himself into his safety harness and told Tami to stay belowdecks where she would be safe.

The hurricane struck and tossed the yacht around like a cork. As Tami closed the door, a large wave descended toward them. It was the last time she saw Richard alive. The boat capsized, and Tami was thrown against a wall and knocked out.

When Tami awoke, she discovered that the masts had broken off and seawater was filling the cabin below deck. Tami had a large gash above her forehead and soon discovered the yacht's navigation and emergency positioning devices were ruined. Most of the other electrical equipment had also been destroyed by seawater. However, she was able to pump out the water flooding the cabin.

There was no time to grieve for Richard or hope for rescue. Tami would have to use all of her strength and sailing experience to survive the shipwreck—entirely by herself.

"The survival instinct is very strong. I wanted to survive; I didn't want to die. It's harder to lie back and hope someone rescues you—I'm more proactive than that—and I'm glad I am because nobody was out there."

HURRICANES

Hurricanes are supercharged storms that occur at sea and gather pace as they speed across warm ocean water. Inside, winds can reach over 150 mph (240 kmh) and unleash torrents of rain.

SURVIVE A SHIPWRECK
- If you do not have an inflatable raft, make a life raft from buoyant objects such as plastic and wood.
- Grab important items from your sinking ship: water, food, flares, a radio, a mirror.
- Stay covered and out of the sun as much as possible to avoid dehydration.

It was not all bad news for Tami aboard the *Hazana*. A search of the cabin revealed a wristwatch and a sextant—tools that would allow her to navigate. She fashioned a small sail using a broken mast, although this only gave the yacht a slow top speed of around 2.3 mph (3.7 kmh). Tami calculated that she was about 1,500 miles (2,400 kilometers) from the islands of Hawaii. She also realized that if she missed the islands, she would be unlikely to survive on the rations of canned fruit and sardines that she had salvaged from belowdecks.

To pass the time, Tami recorded her thoughts in a logbook and counted the days she had survived. She also constantly checked her course. After a while, the yacht struck currents near the equator that made her sail a little faster. However, although Tami tried to stay positive, she was grief-stricken and frightened, and she became depressed after a few weeks. At one point, she saw what she thought was an island, but this turned out only to be clouds. She was once again gripped by excitement when a seaplane flew close by. Tami fired a flare into the sky, but the plane did not see her. She was alone again.

Tami would spend a total of 41 days at sea before glimpsing the island of Hawaii on the horizon. As the crippled yacht made its way toward shore, a Japanese research ship outside Hilo Harbor noticed it and towed it in.

> "While we all rely on electronics and batteries for GPS and handheld radios and all that, I tell you: that sextant saved my life."

After recovering, Tami wrote a book about her experience which was later turned into a movie, *Adrift*. She still sails today near her home on San Juan Island, Washington, and keeps a symbol of her ordeal around her neck: a small pendant in the shape of a sextant.

UNDERGROUND RESCUE

The Chilean Miners

At 2 p.m. on August 5, 2010, vibrations rattled Chile's San José gold and copper mine. There was an explosion, and the mine's tunnels filled with a gritty, choking dust. A 770,000-ton chunk of rock had broken away and fallen into the tunnels that spiraled 2,625 feet (800 meters) below the ground. Now there was no way out.

Above ground, frantic efforts began to find 33 miners who were unaccounted for. Listening probes were lowered down special shafts to detect signs of life. But after 17 days, there were no sounds to indicate anyone had survived.

Then, on August 22, one of the probes detected a faint tapping. When it was drawn to the surface, it brought with it extraordinary news. A note was attached, reading, "All 33 of us are fine in the shelter." A video camera was lowered down and revealed the miners: filthy and shirtless in the heat of the mine. They had holed up in the mine's "refuge": a small tunnel 2,300 feet (700 meters) down, which had emergency supplies of food and water.

The miners had survived the 17 days by eating two spoonfuls of tuna and half a cookie every 24 hours. They were hungry and dehydrated but otherwise unscathed.

Following the discovery, there were great celebrations among the miners' families. But then it was revealed that drilling a rescue hole could take several months. Three different industrial drills would be used to try and reach the refuge. Drilling commenced on August 30.

Hearing that they would be rescued by Christmas, the miners focused on their day-to-day survival. They set up a system for

> "It had a bad taste. It had lots of oil, from the machines, but you had to drink it."
>
> *Miner Richard Villaroel on the water the miners drank*

THE FENIX CAPSULE

Built with help from NASA, the Fenix was a metal rescue capsule that winched the miners to safety one by one. It had audio and video links and even a heart monitor for the ascending miner. A trapdoor and rope were included at the bottom in case the capsule became stuck and the miner needed to escape.

sanitation in an adjoining tunnel and a telephone hub for communication with the outside world. Then they got to work removing fallen debris caused by the drilling and strengthening the walls of the refuge to prevent another collapse. The sound of drilling helped them keep up their morale.

The drilling itself, however, proved to be anything but straightforward. After two months, one drill had drilled only 85 percent of the way down to the refuge. Another drill had drifted off target, and the drill bit of the third drill had even broken off in the rock. The miners became disheartened when they heard the drilling stop.

However, drilling did begin again, and on October 9 the drill broke through into a chamber attached to the refuge tunnel. This hole was then lined with metal tubing to allow a rescue capsule to pass through. Just after midnight, in the early hours of October 13, the first miner was lifted to the surface; by that evening all of the 33 miners had been rescued.

> "To be treated like a rock star—that was stressful. People wanted to touch us. As if we were God, almost."
> *Miner Pedro Cortez on the media attention after the rescue*

Wearing sunglasses against the glare of the light and the cameras, the miners were reunited with their families and taken to a hospital for tests. Physically, there were no lasting effects, but psychologically the ordeal had left scars. More than a billion people had watched their rescue on television, and the miners were invited on media tours around the world. But after the attention faded, several miners became depressed.

In 2011, courts ordered Sernageomin, the company that owns the mine, to compensate the Chilean government for its rescue efforts, but no payment was awarded to the miners.

SURVIVE IN A COLLAPSED MINE

- Ration your food and water.
- Bang on pipes to alert rescuers.
- Establish a system to get rid of your waste products.
- Strengthen your environment against further collapse.

CAUGHT IN A CREVASSE

Douglas Mawson

The first disaster struck Douglas Mawson's team only weeks into their Antarctic trek in 1911. They were there to map the continent's east coast, but blizzards and glaciers hampered their progress. Worse followed when a crevasse suddenly appeared in front of one of the dog-pulled sleds.

Douglas, a British-Australian, had picked army officer Belgrave Ninnis and Swiss mountaineer Xavier Mertz for their skill, strength, and determination. The team set out on November 10, but their high spirits were soon dampened by the weather in the Antarctic region, which is often described as the windiest place on Earth.

The winds around the base camp that Douglas had named Commonwealth Bay seldom fell below 50 mph (80 kmh) and

"That night we ate George. He was a very poor sample; chiefly sinews with a very undesirable taste. It was a happy relief when the liver appeared which, if little else could be said in its favor, could be easily chewed and digested."

sometimes whipped around the team's wooden hut at 185 mph (300 kmh). But the hut was luxurious compared to being out in the snow on dog-pulled sleds for several weeks to map the territory in the east.

The crevasse was partially covered by snow, so Belgrave did not see it until the last moment. He, the sled, and six dogs plunged to the bottom of the crevasse. There was no way to retrieve their bodies, nor the vital supplies that had gone with them. Most of the food for the men, all of the dog food, and the team's main tent were now at the bottom of the chasm.

Douglas and Xavier had 10 days' worth of food, but the journey back to the base camp would take at least four weeks. There was only one solution: they would have to eat the dogs. The men began rationing their food and killing off the dogs one by one, eating the choicest cuts and feeding everything else to the remaining dogs. They thought the livers would give them the most nutrients, but unbeknownst to them, the livers of dogs contain very high levels of vitamin A, a substance toxic to humans when taken at high levels. Before long, both men began to feel ill.

After a few days, the skin around the men's legs began to fall off. They also suffered from crippling stomach cramps and severe diarrhea. Progress was painfully slow, and Xavier became ill, ranting and raving and even breaking a tent pole in anger.

Things reached a climax on January 7, as Douglas described in his journal: "During the afternoon he (Xavier) has several fits and is delirious, fills his trousers again and I clean out for him. He is very weak, becomes more and more delirious, rarely being able to speak coherently." By the evening, Douglas was able to calm Xavier and settle him down into his sleeping bag. By the morning, he had died.

Now alone, Douglas had to travel 100 miles (160 kilometers) to reach his base by January 15—the date his ship was due to depart Antarctica. As he struggled on, the unimaginable happened: he fell into a crevasse. Exhausted and weak, Douglas somehow summoned the strength to find a way back up to the surface. Incredibly, this was only one of several crevasses he fell into and managed to climb out of before reaching camp. As he finally approached the camp, he saw his ship, the *Aurora*, already far out to sea.

Luck, however, was finally on Douglas's side. Six men had remained behind at the camp to wait for him. Unfortunately, the ship could not be recalled, and Douglas had to endure a whole year at the base camp until it came back. Gradually Douglas returned to good physical and mental health, and he returned to Australia a hero a year later.

"Xavier off color. We did 15 miles, halting at about 9 a.m. He turned in—all his things very wet. The continuous drift does not give one a chance to dry a thing, and our gear is deplorable. Tent has dripped terribly, all caked with ice."

SURVIVE IN THE SNOW

- Pack a foldable shovel, thermals, food, water, and an avalanche transceiver (a beacon that helps others locate where you are buried).
- Listen for blizzard watches and avalanche warnings on a portable radio.
- If you're caught in a blizzard, lie down in a dug-out trench that you've lined with branches. Shake off the snow every 30 minutes so you aren't buried.

SPACE DISASTER

Boris Volynov and Soyuz 5

In 1969, Soviet cosmonauts aboard the spacecraft *Soyuz 4* and *Soyuz 5* prepared to make history. They were going to be the first to dock their spacecraft while in orbit around Earth, and then transfer the crew from one craft to another. The operation went without a hitch. That is, until *Soyuz 5* tried to land back on Earth.

The commander of *Soyuz 5* was Boris Volynov, an experienced 34-year-old cosmonaut. He blasted off from Earth aboard *Soyuz 5* on January 16 and then met with *Soyuz 4*, which was already orbiting Earth. The two spacecraft docked together, and two of Boris's crew transferred across to *Soyuz 4*. After four hours and 35 minutes, the spacecraft separated and Boris prepared for his descent to Earth.

Landing back on Earth required the spacecraft's descent module to separate from its service module, which would then be abandoned. As Boris began the landing sequence, he expected to be back on the ground in 30 minutes. But this landing was not going to be routine.

Boris activated the exploding bolts to separate the two modules, but when he looked out of his porthole, he was horrified to see that the service module was still attached—and blocking the

> **"No panic."**
> *A comment from Boris Volynov, heard over the radio during the emergency*

descent module's vital heat shield. Without this protection, both modules were likely to explode in flames as they traveled through Earth's atmosphere.

SOYUZ

Soyuz are the longest-serving crewed spacecraft in history. First launched in 1967 for the Soviet space program, Soyuz spacecraft are still used to today as the main form of transportation to and from the International Space Station.

Boris immediately radioed the news to the Soviet mission control center. But there was nothing they could do to help. As *Soyuz 5* plunged through Earth's atmosphere, fuel tanks on the service module began to explode, causing the hatch on the descent module to buckle inward. Boris could hear a terrible grinding noise as *Soyuz 5* tumbled end over end. Flames scorched the cabin walls.

Boris was not wearing a space suit and could feel the heat burning his face. Outside the spacecraft there was another explosion, and Boris believed his time was up. But all of a sudden, the descent module righted itself and started flying the correct way up. Unbeknownst to Boris, the intense heat from reentry had burned through the cables keeping the service module and the descent module attached. Now the spacecraft's heat shield was doing its job and protecting Boris inside.

Boris immediately wondered where he would land. *Soyuz 5* was now completely off course and headed for the snowy Ural Mountains in Orenburg, Russia. Suddenly there was a violent jolt, and Boris was thrown across the cabin, knocking out several of his teeth. He had landed.

"It's hard to describe my feelings. There was no fear but a deep-cutting and very clear desire to live on when there was no chance left."

However, Boris's troubles were not over. Outside, the temperature was −36°F (−38°C), and it was too cold for Boris to wait for a rescue helicopter. Instead, he walked several miles to the nearest village. The authorities were able to find Boris by the blood and footprints that he left in the snow.

Boris was a national hero for surviving the *Soyuz 5* crash-landing. However, this was not acknowledged until many years later, as his near-miss was kept a state secret until 1997.

SURVIVE IN SPACE

You would perish in minutes without a space suit or spacecraft. Assuming you have one of these, follow these steps:
- Preserve your oxygen; move slowly.
- Ration your food and water.
- Stay warm and calm and await rescue.

THE 2010 HAITI EARTHQUAKE

The 2010 Haiti earthquake killed more than 200,000 people and left more than one million more homeless. The capital Port-au-Prince was flattened in the earthquakes. Digging for survivors lasted for two weeks until the search was called off.

BURIED ALIVE

Evans Monsignac

January 12, 2010, was like any other day for Haitian rice and cooking-oil seller Evans Monsignac. At 5 a.m., he left the one-room apartment that he shared with his two children, wife, and mother, and caught a bus to the marketplace to set up his stall. Then, as Evans sold his last batch of rice, the ground started shaking.

Evans was knocked off his feet, and around him large objects flew through the air. Suddenly, a large piece of concrete pinned Evans down on his right side. He tried to pull to his left, but another piece of concrete fell on him, trapping him completely.

Evans had been caught in one of the most devastating earthquakes ever to strike the small Caribbean island of Haiti. The magnitude 7 earthquake had flattened buildings and cut off electricity and water supplies. Haiti's capital, Port-au-Prince, was the worst affected area. Hundreds of thousands of people had been killed or trapped as buildings collapsed around them. One of them was Evans Monsignac.

> "I'm lying on my back. I was so scared because if I turn one way I will get hurt and if I turn another way I get hurt. If I move it will bring death. So I lay straight."

After the initial tremors had passed, Evans found that he was trapped beneath another slab of concrete. The slab had crashed toward his head but somehow stopped before hitting his face. Now Evans was completely trapped inside a type of concrete

61

SURVIVE AN EARTHQUAKE

- Have an emergency kit with water, food, a cell phone, a battery-powered radio, and a whistle to signal for help.
- Earthquake-proof your home by moving beds away from windows and putting heavy items on lower shelves.
- Have a family plan about where to go and what to do if an earthquake strikes.

tomb. He could hear screams and shouts, and he realized other people were also trapped. But Evans did not dare move. He stayed still on his back and waited.

As time went on, the shouts fell silent. Evans was alive, but he was also alone. He slipped in and out of consciousness as he continued to try to stay still. It was so dark that he was not sure if it was night or day, or how long he had been trapped for.

Around the third day of being trapped, Evans noticed that liquid was trickling past him. He reached his hand down and scooped some into his palm. He brought it toward his mouth and drank. But the liquid was raw sewage. Evans tried not to drink it, but as he got hungrier and thirstier he had no choice. He would rub the foul liquid on his lips, giving him some relief. But the more he drank, the sicker he felt in his stomach.

Many days passed this way. The official search ended, but then, incredibly, Evans was discovered. When the rescuers found Evans, he was showing the signs of severe shock. He was rushed to a nearby field hospital and examined by a doctor, who was astounded when he realized Evans had been trapped for 27 days, surviving only on liquid sewage.

Evans was the last earthquake survivor found, but he was desperately unwell. He had lost 60 pounds (27 kilograms) and was covered in red sores. However, despite being severely dehydrated, Evans had suffered no kidney damage, which was rare for going so long without water. It took many months for Evans to recover, and days for

"The only thing I can remember is thinking 'I'm free, I'm not dying.'"

him to even want to start eating again. But slowly, he began to get better. "I know that I must live life to the best I can each day," Evans said about surviving the Haiti earthquake.

ALL AT SEA

José Salvador Alvarenga

On November 17, 2012, a storm crashed around José Salvador Alvarenga's 23-foot (7-meter) fishing boat. Enormous waves threatened to throw the men inside into the shark-infested waters. As 35-year-old José tried to steer toward land, his crewmate Ezequiel Córdoba bailed out the seawater that was filling the boat.

For hours, the two Salvadorian fisherman battled the storm. The men did not know each other well: Ezequiel was a last-minute replacement for José's regular crewmate, and after a day of weathering the storm he became fearful, convinced they would be eaten by sharks.

Around 9 a.m. the next morning, the two men rejoiced when they saw land. But then the boat's outboard motor stopped working. Waves and a wild swell began pulling the boat back out to sea. Like a roller coaster, the boat would be yanked to the top of the wave one moment before shooting down to the bottom the next. The fish, ice, and gasoline on board were weighing the boat down and making it unstable. José ordered Ezequiel to help him throw everything overboard. Within a few minutes, sharks started circling the boat to eat the fish.

For days, the men battled the storm, taking turns bailing out the water from the boat. By the time the storm passed, the men were far out in the deep waters of the Pacific Ocean.

With their nets and hooks thrown overboard, José fished by leaning over the side of the boat and grabbing fish from the water. Soon the pair were feasting on raw fish and pieces of fish that Ezequiel dried in the sun. But they were terribly dehydrated.

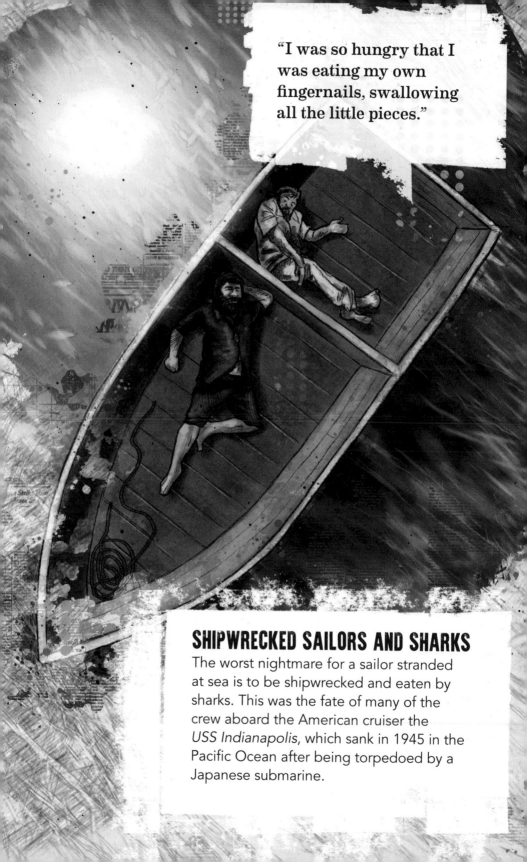

"I was so hungry that I was eating my own fingernails, swallowing all the little pieces."

SHIPWRECKED SAILORS AND SHARKS

The worst nightmare for a sailor stranded at sea is to be shipwrecked and eaten by sharks. This was the fate of many of the crew aboard the American cruiser the *USS Indianapolis*, which sank in 1945 in the Pacific Ocean after being torpedoed by a Japanese submarine.

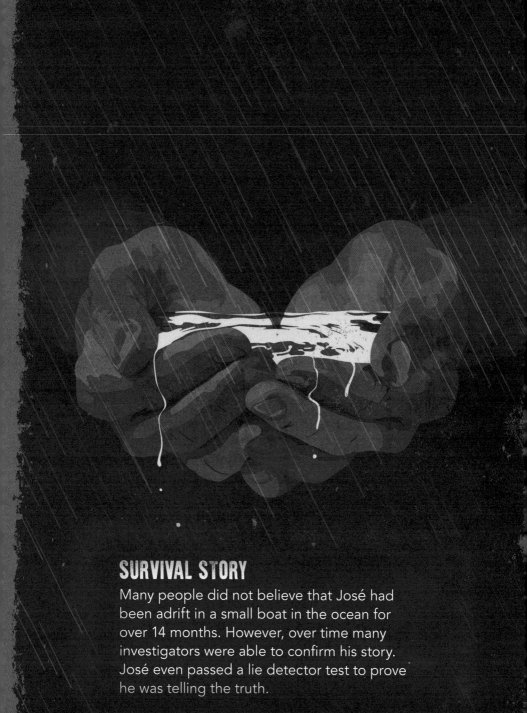

SURVIVAL STORY

Many people did not believe that José had been adrift in a small boat in the ocean for over 14 months. However, over time many investigators were able to confirm his story. José even passed a lie detector test to prove he was telling the truth.

Within days they were drinking their own urine. This gave them some relief, but it made their thirst worse in the long run. However, just when they thought they couldn't go on, clouds appeared overhead and drops of rain began hitting the boat.

The men stripped off and opened their mouths skyward as a deluge of fresh water fell on them from the sky. They were able to collect water in bottles and keep some for later. This gave the men the strength to endure their ordeal. For two months they drifted without rescue.

Eventually, the fear and isolation began to take its toll on Ezequiel. After eating raw seabirds, he had become sick and then refused to eat anything at all. He then stopped drinking water. After a couple of days, Ezequiel lay down and didn't move. Seeing this, José shouted at Ezequiel: "Don't leave me alone! You have to fight for life! What am I going to do here alone?" But by the next morning, Ezequiel was dead. As his body began to decompose, José pushed him into the water and watched him drift away. José was all alone.

As the months passed, José's boat drifted through shipping lanes, but he was unable to attract attention and remained unrescued. He pretended to himself that he was on shore, visiting stores that stocked oranges and fresh tortillas. Then one day he saw seabirds and land on the horizon.

"I was totally destroyed and as skinny as a board. The only thing left was my intestines and gut, plus skin and bones. My arms had no meat. My thighs were skinny and ugly."

After an hour, José had drifted close enough to the tiny island to swim for shore. He staggered along the sand to try and find help. Luckily, the small Tile Islet in the Marshall Islands was inhabited. José was saved. He had drifted, alone at sea, for 438 days.

CLIMBING CATASTROPHE

Joe Simpson and Simon Yates

In 1985, Simon Yates faced an agonizing decision. He was stuck on a ledge while his fallen climbing partner, Joe Simpson, hung from the rope connecting them. But the rope was pulling Simon over the edge. If he didn't cut the rope, both men would fall to their death. By cutting the rope, Simon could at least save himself.

Both Simon and Joe were experienced mountaineers when they decided to climb the 20,000-foot-high (6,000-meter) Siula Grande mountain in the Peruvian Andes. The climbers would need to use a "belaying" rope technique. This meant one climber anchoring themselves to a stable position such as a ledge, while the other climbed. If one of them fell, they would not fall far because they were connected to the anchored climber by their rope.

Simon and Joe's climb to the summit went well, although it took longer than expected. But early into the descent, Joe had an accident, and he slipped down an ice cliff. He broke his right leg and ankle. Simon climbed down to assess the damage and realized that Joe could not climb. He would have to be lowered to the bottom instead.

To do this, Simon tied two lengths of rope together to make one piece, about 300 feet

> "I was the anchor and I was going to be pulled off. Over time, I got colder as I sat on a snow cliff. The snow was collapsing and sooner or later I was going to be pulled off the mountain to my death."
>
> *Simon Yates*

TOUCHING THE VOID

The extraordinary story of Joe Simpson and Simon Yates was widely reported in the media. It was made into a best-selling book called *Touching the Void*, and then into a documentary and a stage play.

CUTTING THE ROPE

When Joe made it back to base camp, Simon was overcome with emotion and worry that he would not get him to a hospital in time. But today Joe says that Simon made the right decision in cutting the rope.

(91 meters) long. He then anchored himself to a ledge and began lowering Joe down. This was complicated and fraught with danger. But neither of them could have anticipated what was about to happen next. As Simon lowered Joe, a storm approached and darkness fell. Simon could not hear Joe calling to him over the noise of the storm, and he lowered him off a ledge by mistake. Joe was now hanging in midair.

There was nothing Simon could do but hope that Joe could climb up the rope. Joe began doing this by creating a Prusik knot, a friction knot that ties two ropes together which can then be used to climb up. But Joe's hands were badly frostbitten, and he dropped one of the ropes. All he could do now was hang there. He waited for over an hour.

Meanwhile, above Joe, Simon was only barely hanging on. The rope was pulling at him and the snow around his belay seat was beginning to slip away. He knew cutting the rope would mean letting Joe fall to his death, but if he didn't, both men would fall. Simon decided to cut the rope. Then he climbed to the bottom by himself, even though he was suffering from hypothermia and severe dehydration.

Meanwhile, Joe woke up to find himself alive. Incredibly, he had survived a fall of 150 feet (45 meters) and landed on a shelf of rock in a crevasse. Joe had to get himself back to base camp alone. He crawled and hopped for 5 miles (8 kilometers) back to the climbers' base camp. In addition to his serious injuries, Joe had had no water or food for three days. It took every last ounce of his strength, but somehow Joe managed to reach the camp alive. Here, Simon had since returned and was preparing to leave. Joe's story of survival quickly became mountaineering folklore.

> "The paradox is that, by cutting the rope, he put me in a position where I could save myself."
>
> Joe Simpson defends Simon Yates's decision to cut the rope.

THE AMAZON

The world's largest tropical rainforest, the Amazon covers almost 2.3 million square miles (6 million square kilometers) of South America. It covers about 4 percent of Earth's land surface, but over half the world's animal and plant species live there.

ALONE IN THE JUNGLE
Juliane Koepcke

Juliane Koepcke and her mother were flying over the Peruvian jungle on New Year's Eve in 1971 when their plane hit turbulence. Luggage was tossed around the cabin, and lightning struck. Then there was a flash by the wing, and Juliane's mother said: "This is it—it's all over." They were the last words Juliane heard her say.

The next thing Juliane remembered was the plane entering a nose dive. The cabin went black, and engines roared loudly. Suddenly, Juliane found herself falling through the air while strapped into her seat, tumbling over and over. She could see the tops of the trees race toward her, and then she blacked out.

Juliane awoke the next morning and realized she had survived an air crash. The plane, she found out later, had broken up more than 2 miles (3 kilometers) above the ground. As far as Juliane could tell, she was the only survivor. The sounds of the jungle filled the air around Juliane, and suddenly she felt very alone.

For someone who had fallen from the sky without a parachute, Juliane had been extraordinarily lucky. Her only injuries were a broken collarbone, a ruptured knee ligament and some cuts. But with her glasses and one shoe missing, Juliane was not equipped for a long jungle trek.

Luckily, Juliane had a working knowledge of the jungle. The teenager had just graduated from high school and had previously lived in the rainforest with her zoologist father and ornithologist mother. She knew that it was the

"The next thing I realized was that I was no longer inside the plane. I was outside. I was sitting in the open air on my seat."

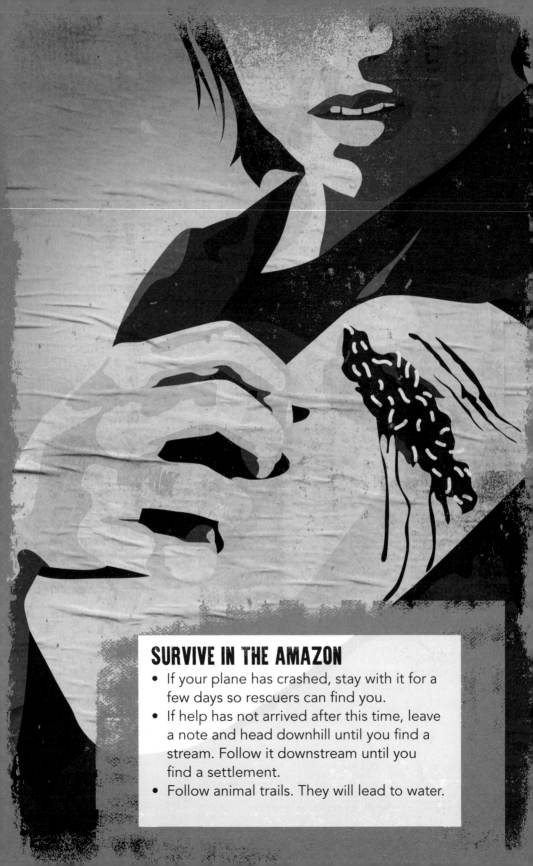

SURVIVE IN THE AMAZON

- If your plane has crashed, stay with it for a few days so rescuers can find you.
- If help has not arrived after this time, leave a note and head downhill until you find a stream. Follow it downstream until you find a settlement.
- Follow animal trails. They will lead to water.

little creatures, such as spiders, ants, and mosquitoes, that she should be most scared of. She also knew that she needed to find a river, which would lead her to a human settlement, and so Juliane set off.

Armed with a bag of candy from the plane, Juliane pushed on through the wet, humid conditions. She walked for 10 days, becoming increasingly weak from hunger. But then the environment began to change, and the creek turned into a river.

Juliane couldn't believe her luck when she saw a boat moored to the riverbank. From the boat, there was a path leading to a hut. Inside was some gasoline. Juliane had noticed while swimming that one of the cuts on her arm was badly infected, and maggots were writhing inside the wound. Juliane sucked out a mouthful of the gasoline and spat it into her wound. The maggots tried to crawl deeper into her flesh, but she pulled them out. In total she counted 30 maggots, all around half an inch (1 centimeter) long.

Exhausted, Juliane stayed the night in the hut. The next morning, she heard men's voices outside. Juliane described the sound as "hearing the voices of angels." The men were startled when she went outside to greet them. She spoke to them in Spanish, explaining what had happened. They then took care of Juliane, giving her food and treating her wounds.

The men took Juliane on their boat to the nearest village and civilization. Her father was lost for words when they were reunited. The body of Juliane's mother was found several days later. Afterward, Juliane moved to Germany and became a librarian.

"I had nightmares for a long time, for years, and of course the grief about my mother's death and that of the other people came back again and again. The thought 'Why was I the only survivor?' haunts me."

SWIM TO SURVIVE

Rosezina Jefferson

In late August 2005, Hurricane Katrina sped toward the south coast of the United States. Residents of New Orleans, Louisiana, were told to evacuate their homes. But heavily pregnant Rosezina Jefferson stayed, thinking the storm "wouldn't be that bad."

As Hurricane Katrina approached the United States, it was a Category 5, the highest rating for a hurricane. The storm weakened slightly as it met land, but it still devastated New Orleans. Torrential rainfall, 120 mph (190 kmh) winds and a huge wall of water quickly broke the city's riverbanks. By August 30, more than 80 percent of the city was underwater.

The floodwater had almost reached the second floor of the apartment that Rosezina and her five-year-old son Ashton were staying in with a friend when Rosezina went into labor. But her more immediate problem was Ashton: he was having an asthma attack and did not have any medicine. On the radio, Rosezina heard that Coast Guard boats were picking up stranded people about half a mile (less than 1 kilometer) away.

Battling labor pains, Rosezina decided to swim for help. She climbed onto the apartment's fire escape and stepped off into the muddy floodwaters. Ashton screamed, "Mama, come back." But Rosezina now had only one choice—to keep swimming.

HURRICANE KATRINA

Hurricane Katrina caused 1,883 deaths and over $108 billion of damage. People from 144,000 households had to be housed in trailers after losing their homes in the disaster.

"I always think about being in labor and leaving my son. I probably would never do that again. I was in labor, and it was a drastic decision."

SURVIVE A HURRICANE
- Find shelter: select a safe, central area away from windows.
- Stay inside and listen to the radio until the all-clear has been given—even if it's calm outside. The eye, or center, of the storm is often calm.
- Don't ever drink floodwater.

Rosezina swam through the churning floodwaters toward the city's interstate highway. As she avoided the cars that floated toward her, Rosezina's labor contractions made her double up in pain. But then she saw a Coast Guard boat coming toward her. Rosezina flagged the boat down and climbed aboard.

Realizing the seriousness of Rosezina's situation, her Coast Guard rescuers radioed for a helicopter to airlift her to a hospital immediately. She was picked up from the boat and flown 75 miles (121 kilometers) to a hospital in Baton Rouge. At 4 a.m. on August 31, Rosezina's second son, Keith, was born.

Rosezina was overjoyed at the birth of a healthy baby but was fraught with worry about the fate of her other son, Ashton. She had left him with her friend in the middle of an asthma attack as the floodwater threatened. What had become of him?

There was no way of returning back to the apartment where Rosezina had left Ashton. All she could do was explain the situation to the authorities and hope and wait. She was not the only person experiencing an emergency.

Although more than a million people had evacuated the city before the hurricane struck, over 100,000 more had stayed put. Now, many of them were missing or stranded as over 10 feet (3 meters) of water covered parts of the city. Within a couple of days there were food and water shortages, and the bacteria in the floodwaters caused a public health emergency.

> "I asked him, did he have faith I'd find him? He just held my hand and smiled."

Soon, 273,000 people were being housed in emergency hurricane shelters. Luckily, one of these people was Ashton, who had recovered from his asthma attack and been evacuated from the apartment building. Three days after she had swum away from the apartment, Rosezina received word that Ashton was safe at a shelter in Houston, Texas.

AMBUSHED BY AN AVALANCHE

Lester J. Morlang

In 1985, Lester J. Morlang and Jack Ritter were outside the mine where they worked when an avalanche struck. High up in the La Plata Mountains, in Colorado, the avalanche came down fast and hard and buried the men under 50 feet (15 meters) of snow. Jack suffocated under this thick layer of "white death." But Lester survived.

Although Lester was trapped deep beneath the snow, an air pocket had formed around his face, enabling him to breathe. But he didn't hold high hopes for his survival. "I had my doubts that I was alive, and I thought I was dead and buried. The only thing I could do is stop and not lose my cool," Lester later said.

Lester used logic to figure out how to help himself. First, he dribbled saliva from his mouth and watched which way it fell. He could then figure out which way was up. He started digging in this direction and didn't stop, digging for nearly 22 hours.

> "The big thing was being able to stay calm. A lot of it was mental. I asked myself, 'Is this how I'm gonna die?' and I decided 'no, it ain't.'"

Lester eventually broke through the final feet of snow and into the open air. It was night by then, and temperatures were well below freezing. To stay alive, Lester built himself a snow cave, which he lined with branches to keep himself off the freezing snow on the ground. He blocked the entrance with branches and tried to build a fire, but he couldn't get his frozen hands to work properly. He lay down and hoped that he would soon be rescued.

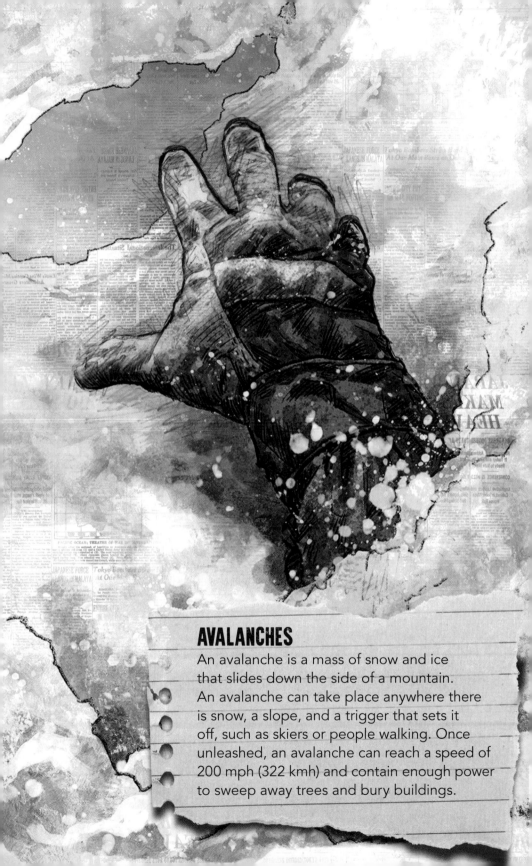

AVALANCHES

An avalanche is a mass of snow and ice
that slides down the side of a mountain.
An avalanche can take place anywhere there
is snow, a slope, and a trigger that sets it
off, such as skiers or people walking. Once
unleashed, an avalanche can reach a speed of
200 mph (322 kmh) and contain enough power
to sweep away trees and bury buildings.

It was then that a second avalanche struck. This time, Lester was buried in less than 3 feet (1 meter) of snow and was able to dig himself out again. He lay on the snow and waited for daybreak.

When dawn came, Lester began heading down the mountain and stopped at a point that was easily visible from the sky. He stamped out "help" into the snow and waited for rescue.

Unbeknownst to Lester, rescuers had been out searching for him and Jack since the day before. Lester heard booms in the distance and realized that rescue teams were using explosives to set off avalanches deliberately, so that they wouldn't cause other avalanches as they searched. In the morning, Lester saw a rescue helicopter fly overhead, but he wasn't sure if it had seen him. A few minutes later, Lester heard a series of explosives being dropped by the helicopter. Then something unimaginable happened—Lester was hit by a third avalanche.

Luckily for Lester, trees kept most of the avalanche snow from covering him, and he was easily able to dig upward and shake himself off. Then, to his delight, the helicopter turned back toward him. "It just tickled me to death to see the helicopter," Lester later said.

Lester's ordeal was not completely over, however. He was dangerously dehydrated and had severe frostbite. He had to have one index finger amputated and the index finger on his other hand partially amputated. For a while Lester needed to use a wheelchair and have his hands and feet bandaged. However, Lester's doctor said it was incredible for him to have survived and that it was his mental strength that had kept him alive.

Over time, Lester made a full recovery and was able to retrain as a truck driver.

AVOID AN AVALANCHE

So you don't set off an avalanche, avoid snow-covered slopes that are:
- Steeper than a playground slide
- Treeless
- Wet or recently rained on.

THE "UNSINKABLE" SHIP

Titanic was built with 16 watertight compartments below deck that could be closed off if any one of them took in water. According to the designers, four of these compartments could fill with water and the ship would still stay afloat. However, the walls dividing the compartments did not go all the way up, so seawater simply sloshed over the compartment walls until the ship sank.

SERIAL SHIPWRECK SURVIVOR

Violet Jessop

Violet Jessop's first shipwreck occurred in 1911. The Irish nurse had taken a job as a stewardess aboard the luxury Atlantic liner the RMS *Olympic*. Owned by the White Star Line, the *Olympic* was the largest civilian ship ever built. Its sister ships were the HMHS *Britannic* and the RMS *Titanic*. Violet would sail on all three.

The *Olympic* began its fifth voyage between Southampton, England, and New York City on September 20, 1911. But as the liner headed out from port, it collided with the war cruiser HMS *Hawke*. The *Hawke* had been specially designed with a steel-reinforced hull to ram enemy ships. It smashed two holes in *Olympic*'s hull. The ship began taking on water but was able to limp back to port. No one was seriously hurt.

"I stood . . . with the other stewardesses, watching the women cling to their husbands before being put into the boats with their children."

Violet describing the scene after Titanic *hit the iceberg*

Violet's next adventure was upon *Titanic*. RMS *Titanic*'s maiden voyage on April 10, 1912, was greeted with much celebration. It was the most luxurious and technologically advanced ship in the world. Tickets were snapped up by the rich and famous who were eager to be a part of this exciting event. Violet had bought herself a nice new brown suit to board the ship in Southampton. The shipmakers were so confident of *Titanic* that they had branded it unsinkable.

This claim was put to the test on April 14, 1912, when *Titanic* collided with a huge iceberg in the Atlantic Ocean. The lookouts had only seen the iceberg floating toward the ship at the last moment. The iceberg scraped along the ship. Freezing seawater gushed through gashes in the ship's side.

Violet was ordered up on deck. Here everyone was told to remain calm. The ship's orchestra played to keep up morale. Many people still believed that the *Titanic* would not sink, even when the captain ordered women and children into the lifeboats. In addition, *Titanic*'s 20 lifeboats could carry only about 1,178 of the 2,000 or so people on board—but when it sank, many of them weren't even full.

One of the lucky ones, Violet was given a place aboard a lifeboat. As the lifeboat rowed away, the ship began to sink lower into the water. *Titanic* sank two hours and 40 minutes after hitting the iceberg. Violet's lifeboat was picked up the next morning by the RMS *Carpathia*. Violet had survived, but more than 1,500 people had been killed.

In 1916, Violet was working as a nurse aboard the HMHS *Britannic*, which had been converted into a hospital ship. On November 21, the ship hit a mine and began to sink. This was Violet's third shipwreck—and the most dangerous yet. Her lifeboat was sucked toward the ship's propellers and she had to jump into the water, hitting her head in the process. However, Violet once again survived and continued to work aboard ships until the 1950s, when she retired to dry land in Suffolk, England.

"I leapt into the water but was sucked under the ship's keel, which struck my head. I escaped, but years later when I went to my doctor because of a lot of headaches, he discovered I had once sustained a fracture of the skull!"

The sinking of the HMHS Britannic

MULTIPLE SURVIVORS

Arthur John Priest, a stoker who fed the ships' boilers with coal, also survived the three shipwrecks that Violet did. He even survived two further shipwrecks aboard the RMS *Asturias* and HMS *Donegal*. He died of old age in 1937 on dry land.

Timeline

Violet Jessop survives the first of three shipwrecks.

1911

1911

1969

Douglas Mawson survives several weeks trekking across Antarctica after the rest of his team perish.

Cosmonaut Boris Volynov survives a spacecraft malfunction during reentry to Earth.

1971

Juliane Koepcke survives a plane crash and 11 days in the Amazon rainforest.

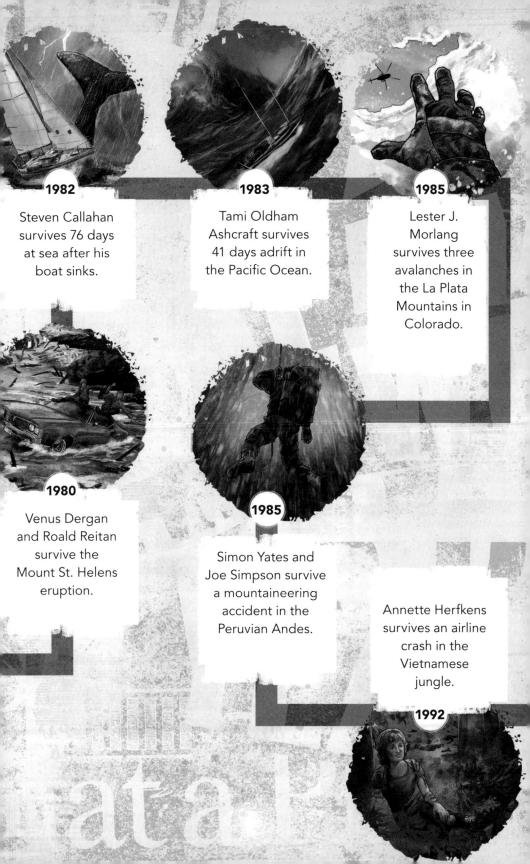

1982

Steven Callahan survives 76 days at sea after his boat sinks.

1983

Tami Oldham Ashcraft survives 41 days adrift in the Pacific Ocean.

1985

Lester J. Morlang survives three avalanches in the La Plata Mountains in Colorado.

1980

Venus Dergan and Roald Reitan survive the Mount St. Helens eruption.

1985

Simon Yates and Joe Simpson survive a mountaineering accident in the Peruvian Andes.

Annette Herfkens survives an airline crash in the Vietnamese jungle.

1992

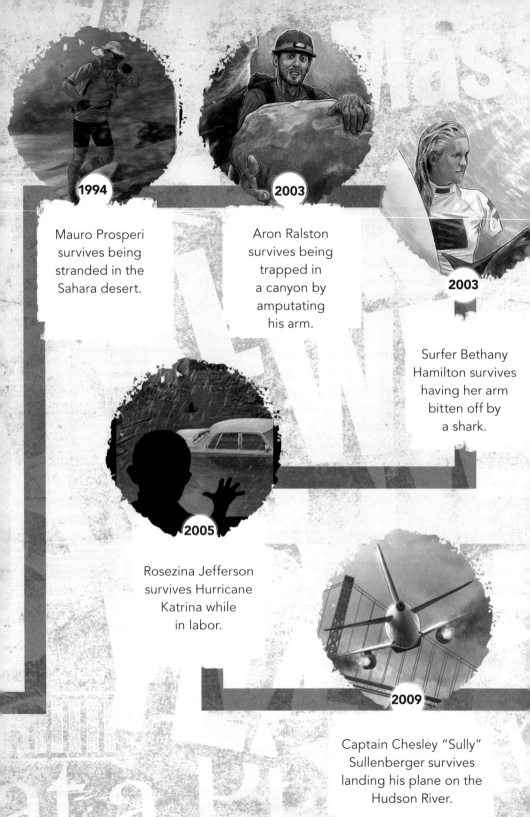

1994

Mauro Prosperi survives being stranded in the Sahara desert.

2003

Aron Ralston survives being trapped in a canyon by amputating his arm.

2003

Surfer Bethany Hamilton survives having her arm bitten off by a shark.

2005

Rosezina Jefferson survives Hurricane Katrina while in labor.

2009

Captain Chesley "Sully" Sullenberger survives landing his plane on the Hudson River.

2018

Allyn Pierce survives an evacuation during the California wildfires.

2018

The Wild Boars soccer team survives the flooded Tham Luang cave.

2012

José Salvador Alvarenga is caught in a storm that keeps him stranded at sea for 438 days.

2010

The Chilean miners survive being trapped underground for 69 days.

2010

Evans Monsignac survives under earthquake rubble in Haiti for 27 days.

Quiz

How much can you remember about the survivors in this book? Take this test to find out. Answers are on page 96.

1. What did Steven Callahan think his _Napoleon Solo_ boat had collided with?
a) A whale   b) A dinghy   c) A mine

2. Who played Captain Chesley Sullenberger in the survivor movie _Sully_?
a) Al Pacino   b) Bill Murray   c) Tom Hanks

3. What did the Berber women give Sahara survivor Mauro Prosperi to drink?
a) Bat's blood   b) Goat's milk   c) Urine

4. Why were Venus Dergan and Roald Reitan camping near Mount St. Helens?
a) To observe the eruption
b) Because Venus had just been made homeless
c) They were on a fishing trip

5. What category was the hurricane that struck Tami Oldham Ashcraft's yacht?
a) 3   b) 4   c) 5

6. How heavy was the boulder that landed on Aron Ralston's arm?
a) 265 lb.   b) 350 lb.   c) 800 lb.

7. How old was Wild Boar team member Peerapat turning on Saturday, June 23, 2018?

a) 16   b) 17   c) 18

8. Where in Vietnam was Annette Herfkens traveling to when her plane crashed?

a) Ho Chi Minh City   b) Nha Trang   c) Hanoi

9. What did Boris Volynov say to himself when he realized his *Soyuz 5* had malfunctioned?

a) "I'm going to die."   b) "Is this the end?"   c) "No panic."

10. What is the name of Rosezina Jefferson's eldest son?

a) Ashleigh   b) Anthony   c) Ashton

11. On what date in 1971 was Juliane Koepcke involved in a plane crash?

a) Christmas Day   b) New Year's Eve   c) Easter Sunday

12. What kind of shark bit off Bethany Hamilton's arm?

a) Tiger shark   b) Great white   c) Bull shark

13. What did Evans Monsignac sell at his stall?

a) Rice and oil   b) Oil and beans   c) Tools and screws

14. What is one of the main causes of avalanches?

a) Loud noises   b) People   c) Brown bears

15. What vitamin made Douglas Mawson and Xavier Mertz ill?

a) Vitamin A   b) Vitamin B   c) Vitamin C

Glossary

Amputate to cut off a limb.

Berber a member of the native people of North Africa, such as the nomadic Tuareg.

Camcorder a small video recorder for making home movies.

Capsize to overturn, usually in heavy seas.

Colleague a workmate or coworker.

Cosmonaut a Russian astronaut.

Decompose to become rotten.

Delirious a confused state of mind accompanied by illusions and incoherent rambling.

Ditching the controlled emergency landing of a plane on water.

Hull the main body of a ship, including its bottom, sides, and deck.

Ornithologist an expert on birds.

Magnitude the destructive power of an earthquake, from 1–10.

Projectile a missile that flies through the air with great force.

Sanitation providing clean water and sewage disposal.

Scorch to burn a surface, making its color brown and black.

Sloop a type of yacht that has one mast.

Soviet belonging to the Soviet Union, the collection of 14 communist states that included Russia.

Tourniquet a bandage that stops the flow of blood.

Trawler a type of fishing boat that uses nets.

Turbulence an unsteady movement of air causing bumpiness on airplanes.

White death the name mountaineers give to avalanche snow.

Answers

1. a: Steven Callahan thought his boat had collided with a whale.

2. c: Tom Hanks played Captain Chesley Sullenberger in the movie.

3. b: The Berber women gave Mauro Prosperi goat's milk to drink.

4. c: Venus Dergan and Roald Reitan were on a fishing trip.

5. b: The hurricane was a Category 4 storm.

6. c: The boulder that landed on Aron Ralston's arm weighed 800 lb.

7. b: Peerapat was turning 17.

8. b: Annette Herfkens was traveling to Nha Trang.

9. c: Boris Volynov said, "No panic."

10. c: Rosezina Jefferson's eldest son is named Ashton.

11. b: Juliane Koepcke's plane crashed on New Year's Eve.

12. a: A tiger shark bit off Bethany Hamilton's arm.

13. a: Evans Monsignac sold rice and oil.

14. b: People are one of the main causes of avalanches.

15. a: Vitamin A made Douglas Mawson and Xavier Mertz ill.